# A SHEPHERD'S STORY

## Shadows of Death to God's Glory

## BY LEIVON CANARY KOM

A Shepherd's Story

Shadows of Death to God's Glory

Leivon Canary Kom

2023© by Leivon Canary Kom

## BIBLE SCRIPTURES

Printed in the United States of America

Spirit Media and our logos are trademarks of
Spirit Media

# ❧ SPIRIT MEDIA

www.spiritmedia.us
1249 Kildaire Farm Rd STE 112
Cary, NC 27511
1 (888) 800-3744

Kindle Store › Kindle eBooks ›
Religion & Spirituality Books ›
Christian Books & Bibles › Christian Living

Paperback ISBN: 978-1-958304-20-4
Hardback ISBN: 978-1-958304-21-1
Audiobook ISBN: 978-1-958304-23-5
eBook ISBN: 978-1-958304-22-8
Library of Congress Control Number: 2023900754

# Register This New Book

Benefits of Registering*

- FREE replacements of lost or damaged books
- FREE audiobook—*Get to the Point* by Kevin White
- FREE information about new titles and other freebies

spiritmedia.us/register

*See our website for requirements and limitations

*I choose to dedicate this book to my beloved parents because they disciplined me to be a better man and also to the friends who helped me to fulfill my wishes of writing this book.*

# PREFACE

As I was writing this book, I made every possible effort to be brief with the purpose of communicating the things I so much desire to share with others.

Whatever strands of information that are uppermost in my mind come first. I avoided writing a piece of content in this book like an essay as much as possible, and I lined up the strands of information separately, but all connected end to end.

God is so good. He blesses all humans in different ways. I wrote this book to share my story and encourage poor people like me wherever my voice can't go to testify of God.

We are His. So, we don't need to worry about anything in life. The only thing that matters is to trust and obey Him.

This book is all about myself being hopeful when my situation is hopeless.

I like to share my story with others who are suffering physically and spiritually.

And this book is not the work of one person but a combination of several persons from India and America. We express thanks to the thousands of brothers and sisters in Christ from around the world who have kept a copy of this book. To Christ be the glory forever and ever! Amen!

*Leivon Canary Kom*

# ACKNOWLEDGEMENT

I never even imagined in my wildest fantasies that I would write a book. Life just went on, and at long last, I wrote a book on "GOD'S LOVE," through the inspiration and empowerment of my spiritual Mom Barbara Hemphill Taylor, Raleigh, North Carolina. She was the initial source of inspiration and the igniting force for me to write this book. The second was Aunt Brenda Quine Heintzelman along with others too numerous to mention who helped me to write this book. And the third was the publishers, Spirit Media. They helped me to publish the book successfully in almost no time.

I trust that this book will testify of GOD'S LOVE, giving you health, happiness, truth, and peace.

*Leivon Canary Kom*

# CONTENTS

# CONTENTS

# CHAPTER 1

## MY HOMELAND MANIPUR

My sweet and never-to-be-forgotten homeland 'Manipur' is one of the most beautiful show-places in the world. It is the habitat of countless species of flora and fauna. And what is more interesting, Manipur is the abode of a unique flower that is locally known as Shirui Lily. Shirui Lily is a rare and famous flower that is only growing in Shirui peak, Ukhrul District. Shirui Lily is rare because it cannot be transplanted anywhere else in the world.

*Shirui Lily, famous flower that is only growing in Shirui peak, Ukhrul District.*

In the old days, Manipur used to be as happy as a paradise, peaceful and secure, but not anymore. Manipur was compared to many other breathtaking parts of the world, thus being described in sweet and lovely ways by the great leaders from India and other countries who saw the beauties of its nature.

I won't be wrong in saying that Manipur was just

like the Garden of Eden that the serpent spoiled. Satan has jeopardized it through the selfish minds of people. In fact, most of its population is under the absolute control of Satan. Thou shalt not kill, says the Bible. But selfish people have made Manipur a killing field.

God doesn't want anyone to die. But here in Manipur, selfish people kill their family and friends to get what they want. Almost everybody is running after the things of Satan when they are supposed to be doing God's commands.

Today, God is warmly, cordially, and earnestly inviting every citizen of Manipur to come and reason together with Him as well as giving them the sad story of Satan's rebellion and fall. He is distinctly informing everyone to obey Him so that none of them will be in trouble.

But almost everybody is ignoring Him because they love worldly pleasures more than Him.

No matter how risky the situation of Manipur is, I am most confident that God will be faithful to His chosen people, keeping them safe and secure from all kinds of evil throughout their physical and spiritual journey.

Those who aspire to do good and right often seem to fail, as they become the target of selfish people. It is so sad that many professing people of God, too, are so busy running businesses or doing unBiblical things! Even many leaders are carried away by the selfishness and greediness of this environment. Can a heart full of dirty politics be filled with the fruit of the Holy Spirit? Not at all.

So, dear friend, if you are in a similar situation, never give up your faith in God. Manipur may be gone forever, but you don't have to be. Keep trusting in His promises. The time will surely come when Jesus gives you the reward of doing His Father's will and the crown of glory and everlasting life. Keep walking toward your destination. Never give up! Never!

# CHAPTER 2

## MY BIRTH AND BEHAVIOR

I was born in a nominally Christian family on March 19, 1985, which has a Baptist Christian history from my paternal grandad's side. We are seven siblings, four brothers and three sisters. One of my brothers is the eldest child in our family. The second, third, and fourth are my sisters. I am the fifth. The sixth and seventh are my younger brothers.

*Leivon Canary Kom, I was born in a nominally Christian family on March 19, 1985.*

From the moment I began to understand things better as a child, I could also understand the love and will of God and the purposes of His making me in my mother's womb and my birth.

In other words, I never spoke against the Bible and never will, never did anything that is against God's will, and never will.

Nobody has ever told me that God has a purpose in my birth, but the still small voice has. I wasn't born with a golden spoon. I don't mind that because God had a different plan for my birth family and has a unique purpose for me.

My parents and grandparents used to say that wherever they put me to sit as a toddler, such as on a table or chair, I would sit still until they came back. Whatever they told me to do, I would do it.

In a nutshell, I love my village and miss it. I've been gone for twenty-one years now. It is tiny and needy beyond description.

Elders say that the village has a history of over a hundred years. But even today, it is still the same old environment. Who is to blame for this misfortune? The future will reveal the cause.

There are no signs of education, development, and prosperity in the village yet. I grew up in that underprivileged village.

Since 2000, God has been taking me to different parts of India as His servant. Not as a pastor but as a daily bread earner. He enables me to share His love and plan of salvation with others all the time while doing my jobs. And to this day, I still do so.

I keep hoping and praying that I will be doing bigger things for His kingdom in the future.

# CHAPTER 3

My parents were daily wage laborers. Their strength and dignity lay in the sweat gathered on their brows as they struggled to earn bread for every day. They would work long hours in the woods and fields amid hot and cold weather every day, like cattle .

Unfortunately, their blood, toil, tears, and sweat were no better than a way to get one-day meals.

That too, plain foods, and not sumptuous ones. No matter how miserably they live, I am so thankful that they live as God says in Genesis 3:19 (BRG) "In the sweat of thy face shalt thou eat bread, till thou return unto the ground; for out of it wast thou took: for dust thou art, and unto dust shalt thou return."

"For I know the thoughts that I think toward you, saith the LORD, thoughts of peace, and not of evil, to give you an expected end." Jeremiah 29:11 (BRG).

I wouldn't have seen this beautiful world if it hadn't been for my parents. I regard them with all due respect and love as deities that I can see with my physical eyes. Even though we didn't have enough to eat daily, they always gave us something to eat.

They don't have any relatives who are big shots to support or speak for them. What they have are only ordinary people. Nevertheless, God has better plans for their welfare and not for evil.

# CHAPTER 4

## MY MOTHER'S BUSINESS AND DESIRES

I still vividly remember my mother always carrying one big bag with either side of her hands that fit some different traditional sarongs and another gigantic basket of a kind of fermented fish (Rimse in Kom pronounced as Reem-say, or henthak in Manipuri pronounced as hayn-thuhk) for sale.

*Rimse in Kom, my mother products.*

She was an expert in making this food. I surely do miss eating it. In some seasons she would sell Kom, Meitei, and Mizo, traditional sarongs, carrying them on foot to towns several miles away. Sometimes I would accompany her, but she didn't have me carry any heavy stuff except an umbrella. Sometimes, one of my older sisters would go with her. And at other times, one of my younger brothers would do so.

All these past events of my walking and talking and laughing with my mother are still fresh in my mind. It seems like they happened just yesterday, although they happened many years ago.

My love for my mother is a zillion times bigger than the universe, but I am forever disappointed that a hundred-mile distance and time didn't allow me to see her for the last time when she lay down in her coffin, crossing over out of this sinful world!

I will never forget the six things that she used to tell us:

1. Never forget what people did for you.

2. Learn to forgive others.

3. When people criticize you, you will never die.

4. Never fight with anybody.

5. Never forget what the Bible says.

6. If you want God and man to be happy with you, be generous.

# CHAPTER 5

## THE BOOKS THAT I GOT TO READ

The first book that I ever fell in love with was the Holy Bible in King James Version. My paternal grandad, Leivon Ringlersong Kom, always said that the Holy Bible is where God speaks to man and gives him all the information that he needs for the welfare of his physical and spiritual life.

*Holy Bible in King James Version, the first book that I ever fell in love with.*               *Credit: Google Images*

So, I grew interested in this book after hearing what my grandad would say about it. When I first began reading it, I didn't know all the words in every verse. But through the situational contexts and guidance of the Holy Spirit, I could sense the central ideas.

At age thirteen, I began studying the Bible in King James Version by praying to God every day.

To understand every chapter and verse in the English Bible in King James Version, I would do many types of research on the English language by juxtaposing the Manipuri Bible and Anglo-Manipuri grammar books.

In doing so, I became a bookworm. Back then, if I didn't get to read a book during the day, I couldn't sleep at night. I had read even the books that B.A. and M.A. students studied before I started going to school. I got all these books and other books like novels from my youngest maternal aunt, Mangte Nungsithoi Kom.

People spent many thousands of rupees on learning things, whereas I spent almost no rupees on it. God didn't let anybody support me financially when I was growing up, but he provided me with different ways. But all things considered, I am beyond thankful to God that He has helped me understand His purposes!

# CHAPTER 6

## THE MIRACLES THAT GOD HAS SHOWN ME

In the past, God has shown me several miracles. They testified of His existence to me. I shall put three of them in the record.

**FIRST MIRACLE**

Way back in March of 1994 God healed me from my severe fever. My parents asked an uncle and his wife to take me to the remote village (Chingai)

31

in Ukhrul where my older brother and his sons were working as timber carriers. Their purpose in sending me there was to get some money from my brother to meet family needs.

On the evening we reached the village, I got seriously sick with a fever. That night, I went to bed without having dinner or even a cup of boiled water because I had a bitter mouth, a loss of appetite, and couldn't dump down anything into my tummy. The uncle and aunt who took me were so worried because there were no medicines or pharmacies available at that time.

Through some other workers that were going back into their workplace in the woods, my uncle messaged my brother.

As it dawned, I woke up still sick. I got up, kept the window open to get fresh air in, and knelt on the bed to pray for God's healing touch. As I was praying, I felt as if the rays of God's power were reflecting all over my body from head to toe. My sickness was gone instantly. Then, I ended my prayer. When I opened my eyes, the rays of the rising sun were shining into the room through the open window .

A few minutes later, my brother came running with some medicines, like paracetamol and stoppage. When he saw me standing outside the house, he asked why I was standing there when I was sick, because he didn't know that my sickness was gone. I told him and the people who were there at that moment the whole story of what happened to me as I was praying. But they didn't take me seriously.

My brother gave me the medicines to take, but I didn't use them. I believe God is a doctor everywhere, even where there are no doctors and no medicines.

## SECOND MIRACLE

One Sunday morning in June of 1997, I climbed up a mountain in my village for fasting and prayer. I was praying  to receive God's blessings, such as guidance, assurance, protection, intervention, forgiveness, humility, health, wisdom, comfort, strength, hope, victory, joy, peace, and other needs.

At about 8 o'clock, I began my program with a short prayer.

Then, I studied the book of Psalms for several hours. Then I prayed about all those things that I mentioned above.

After that, I studied the book of Proverbs, which is one of my favorite Scriptures. As I was in the middle of studying it, suddenly the sky darkened, and it started to thunder.

Just then, I knelt and prayed, 'Dear God, please don't let it rain over here, or else my Bible and I will get drenched.'

As I was praying, I could hear that it started to rain at a distance from me. I kept asking God not to let it rain over me, and I prayed as long as it rained.

Sometime after it stopped, I ended my one-hour-long prayer. Miraculously, my Bible and I didn't even get one drop of rain.

To my great surprise, when I ran around and looked, I found out that a circle with a diameter of 10 meters where I prayed wasn't wet!

## THIRD MIRACLE

One day in July of 1997, as the vehicles were off the roads, some friends and I had to take the foot-track on a hill (Wangoupalon) to reach the Head Quarters Chandel for an Indian Army Recruitment Rally.

This mountain has been the abode of gods and goddesses. They have killed many people, young and old.

When we reached the top of this mountain, it started thundering. It thundered a few times, then started drizzling. It drizzled for some time, then started fogging. But it didn't rain heavily, just drizzling.

Within a few seconds, my shoes got covered with mud. I could barely walk.

As soon as I finished bending down to take off my shoes and tried to stand up, I felt as if someone held me back tightly.

I couldn't stand up, but when I uttered Jesus' mighty name, I was set free.

The deity let go of me in fear of Jesus' mighty name and the Bible tract, which was in my backpack. I was exceedingly glad that the guardian angels of God rescued me from his clutch.

Then, I ran toward my friends as fast as I could until I caught up with them. I saw them waiting for me at some distance, probably around one hundred and thirty yards away.

That same night, the scene of the deity holding me back so tightly appeared in my dream. As he saw the Bible tract that was in my backpack, he set me free. Just then, the female deity came and asked, 'Why did you let go of him?'

They tried to catch me when I was flying up into the sky, but they couldn't do so.

That Incident is forever etched in my mind and still strengthens me physically and spiritually as I am growing in wisdom and knowledge of God.

# CHAPTER 7

As far as my early education goes, at age three, my mom began teaching me the basic skills of reading and writing Manipuri. Sometimes my dad would teach me, too. I didn't study from Grade 1 to 4 due to my parents' extreme poverty.

At age five, I started my schooling directly in Grade 5 on passing a test in a private school, Bethany English School (now as ANK English Academy School), Langmeidong, Thoubal District, Manipur. I took my tenth Grade exam under the name of Langmeidong Higher Secondary School.

And six months later, I dropped out of school due to my parents' inability to pay my school bill.

And nine years later, I studied again in the same old school in the hopes that I would be able to work for the kingdom of God in the future. By then, I got enrolled directly in Grade 9 on passing a test.

I passed my 10th Grade Exam in the year 2000. But unfortunately, my parents' financial situation never improved. I had no other choice than to drop out of college while studying in Grade 11.

From then on, I quit college forever, and what I desired to be as a student was lost.

But I continued teaching myself through voracious reading under the guidance of the Holy Spirit, and still do so.

I always thank and praise God that He blessed me to read and understand the English Bible in King James Version within three weeks after learning. This happened before I went back to the same old school for my further education.

I live below the poverty line in the bush, living a poor local traditional life. That's why I couldn't come up in life at the wrong time. Nevertheless, I know for a fact that God has never forsaken me and that He has better plans in store for me.

Long story short, I went to school only two and a half years in my life.

# CHAPTER 8

## MY TEACHING MINISTRY

Ever since I could read and write things in Hindi, Manipuri, and English, I've been teaching others young and old for free. I still do so. And besides that, I have been doing a lot of social activities as well.

I feel strongly about the teaching ministry because we can access the young minds of the learners and their families, using education to share the word of God.

I have taught in several private schools that are under the Governments of the regions for fourteen years as a teacher of English, Mathematics and Science from Grade two to ten, although I took my schooling for only two and a half years.

All the schools that I taught in are non-profit hunting institutions run by volunteers and like-minded people. The school bills and teachers' salaries are not much. The names of the schools in which I taught and my duration of service are as follows:

*Cannibals' English School, Pangaltabi, Thoubal District. (The year 2000). Service during my Grade eleven. Manipur.*

*Grace Reach Academy, Hiyanglam, Thoubal District. (2001). Manipur.*

*TMT School, Chandel District. (2002-3; 2007-8 & 2010). Manipur.*

*Shalom Matriculation School, Kanchipuram District,(2005), Tamil Nadu.*

*Vision Unique School, Ukhrul District. (2011-2014). Manipur.*

*Kiddies' School, Ukhrul District. (2015-2016). Manipur.*

I have thousands of students in India and Burma, most of whom are non-Christians. Everyone loves me. Some of them consider me as their best teacher. However, if it comes to religion, pretty much everyone gets put off. Anyhow, I planted the seeds of the divine truth into their hearts. Prayerfully, the Holy Spirit will do the rest.

I always pray that God will give me a school and a Church so that I can teach His lessons of truth to others for as long as I live in this world!

I am so sad that there are many people all over the world that haven't yet heard the name of our Savior, even online, although His testimony has come such a long way since two thousand years ago!

But the name of a movie star is known to almost every person in the world. For example, the Chinese actor named Bruce Lee is known even to every kindergarten student on the planet. He's not a God. Yet, everyone recognizes him.

# CHAPTER 9

My childhood memories are ever-to-be-remembered stories combined with sadness and happiness.

I distinctly remember all those days and activities! My one sweetest childhood memory is that my lost mother would kiss me and hug me to her bosom over filial love and affection when I did or said good things.

*Leivon Sumtinnei Kom, my mother.*

My other fondest memory is that my parents, siblings, and I would eat 'Theipuibo Singsu (spicy salad-like food. Its ingredients are salt, garlic, fermented fish and fresh vangueria Spinosa leaves) and Bu'(rice), Awathapi Singsu (fresh papaya singsu) and Bu, and various other edible tree leaves when we worked so hard in hot weather, with buckets of sweat in the woods and fields.

My other fondest memory is that my second younger brother, Mangneisong, and I would do many good jobs together as if we were friends, such as catching crabs and fish in seasons, setting traps for birds and animals, foraging wild mushrooms, hunting wasps on the high hills and down the steep slopes, shooting birds with catapults, and all that.

Back in the day, he was my best friend, and I was his best friend. We were always together. I loved him so dearly. I still do so, although we have gone different ways for twenty-one years now.

After not seeing each other for all these years, I am somewhat disappointed to see that he is not as close and open to me now as he used to be. Neither are my other siblings.

Indeed, the poverty and misunderstanding between us have separated us from our relationships. But, the birds and animals that grew together in one place live together and even die together. However, in my case, I still am the same old myself to them, and I have always prayed for them. I always will.

And my other sweetest memory is that my second older sister, named Rosmi, and I would wake up at dawn and go over the distant paddy fields to pick up the grains that fell to the ground and gather sheaves that the landowners left at harvest time. We also used to take contracts from paddy field owners to cut the grain stalks for them. They would give us some bags of grain in return.

For all those precious lessons of life, I am most thankful to God who brought me into this world to do His WILL and not the world's DEMANDS.

# CHAPTER 10

## MY REGRETS AND MISTAKES

Regrets and mistakes are inseparable parts of life. Every person on earth has regrets and mistakes. And so do the other creatures of God, such as birds and animals. Even God does have regrets from time to time. There are several Biblical examples of His regrets, such as Gen 6:5-7; Ex 32:6-14; I Sam 15:10-11; II Sam 24:15-16; Psalm 106:40-45.

He, indeed, has regrets about doing some things even though He knew beforehand that they wouldn't work out. But His personality and emotions are infinitely more complex than ours and are not limited in the ways that ours are.

Besides, He doesn't lie or change His mind because He is not a man that changes his mind. We humans feel great regret and remorse over our discipline that results in the Holy Spirit running away from us.

And yet, we feel that our discipline and behavior are correct, although we know that they will give us heartache later on.

Speaking of myself, I have a ton of regrets and mistakes about doing things that I WISH I hadn't done. I'd like to lay just a few here:

When I was little, I was growing so fast. I had big legs and hands. I grew faster than my peers and elders in the village. My older sisters, friends, neighbors, and relatives called me an elephant because of my big body size. They would tell me that I would already grow into a gigantic and foolish man before I went to school. They used to make fun of me!

Little did I know back then that being tall and big is super helpful for life. None of my sisters, friends, or relatives encouraged me to have a good stature. None of them told me the importance of growing tall and big enough because they didn't know it, either. Instead, they would say, 'Don't eat so much. Food is scarce.'

From continually hearing their negative remarks, I became self-conscious and ashamed of myself for growing faster than the other boys of my age.

So, I decided not to eat much any more, to delay and control my physical growth. When I studied in Grade nine and ten, I went to school without eating breakfast, morning meals, or any junk food for two years. I would eat only dinner.

It was my foolishness that I didn't eat enough of the plain food that my poor parents could afford to feed us, or sleep enough since burning the midnight oil every night because I aspired to be a man of letters.

Too late, I realized all these things stunted my physical growth and the advantages of having good stature! When I turned thirteen years old, I was 5.5 feet tall (167.64 cm tall). I didn't grow taller than this height.

Nevertheless, I receive comfort and peace from 1 Sam 16:7 (BRG) "But the Lord said unto Samuel, Look not on his countenance, or on the height of his stature; because I have refused him: for the Lord seeth not as man seeth; for man looketh on the outward appearance, but the Lord looketh on the heart."

And nothing can ever stunt my spiritual growth!

# CHAPTER 11

## MY BIBLE MINISTRY

Ever since my childhood days, I've been doing all kinds of ministries for my family, friends, relatives, neighbors, and others regardless of their caste, creed, color, and religion whenever I feel obligated to do so, because God brought me into this world to minister to all of His creatures for His kingdom and glory.

I have given my time, talents, and resources to others. Every time I serve people who need me, I find the greatest joy and most fulfillment in the life purposes that God gave me.

There is still a lot more in my heart that I have always wanted to do to promote the gospel of Christ at the unreached places.

Many Churches and Christian individuals are continually donating money for extending the kingdom of God through Charity Foundations and others besides.

I have always heard about several Christian projects in India. Yet, many of these projects are misusing the donated funds, benefiting the friends and relatives of the administrators but not the very people they are meant to help.

That's why many Indians haven't heard the name of Jesus yet, although His love message arrived in India shortly after He ascended to His Father.

Thanks to the progress in Science and Technology today, it is harder than ever to embezzle the funds of God like they used to.

However, it is not too much to say that Satan has been controlling the finances since two hundred decades ago.

So, we should be careful to make donations only to Foundations and Organizations in the name of Christ that we have researched.

God sees everything. He knows my heart because He created me. I would ask Him to let me do what I feel willing enough to do for others, especially for underprivileged people like me. But He would always tell me that my name was on the waiting list.

After many years' wait, He began to fulfill my wishes one by one.

For instance, He had my father and me hand out Bibles to needy Christian friends and Hindu friends during the Covid-19 lockdown. He provided us Bibles and other empowerments through Mom Barbara.

# CHAPTER 12

I feel led to share some snippets of points on this topic. We ought to understand all the administrative systems of the physical and spiritual world.

The total percentage of Christians in the world is currently 31, Islam is 24, Hindu is 15, and Secular is 15.

Likewise, India's population is 80% Hindu, 13% Islam, 2% Christian, and 0.27% secular.

The Holy Spirit is so sad to have only 2% of Christians in this big country since 52 AD! Even this 2% is not all for Christ. The majority out of 2% are on and off Christians. They go to church and claim to be Christians just because their parents are Christians or Pastors or Church leaders or Association leaders.

That is one of the chief reasons why there is almost no progress in Indian Christianity. I have even seen many Indian Christians converting to Hinduism. I am so distressed and frustrated to see them falling into Satan's temptations and traps!

As God is witness, there have been inner corruptions among the Indian Christian leaders and members. Of course, they pray that God will give them new leaders to lead them, but they don't pray for what God needs, only for their selfish gains. I am so sad about their Christless behaviors and leadership qualities. Everybody knows that Social, Political, and Religious Systems that are Godless are dangerous.

Hinduism is the world's oldest religion that dates back about 4,000 years. With over 900 million Hindus in India, Hinduism is the third-largest religion behind Christianity and Islam in the world. Most of the world's Hindu people live in India.

So, we must live our everyday lives, allowing God to be with us in their midst. If we don't, trouble can come our way at any time. The saddest thing is, many Indian Christian leaders and members are getting trapped in Indian politics nowadays.

At the time of an election, if the wrong candidate gives them an attractive package of money with many false promises, they vote for him. Christians have killed each other just for some selfish purposes. And so do even the families and relatives. All these unChristian actions are under the remote control of Satan.

Just think about this: Jesus would have had support if He had wanted to overthrow the existing powers. But He didn't want to get involved in politics. Instead, He taught peace and non-violence. Paul said to this one, "Remind them to submit to rulers and authorities, to obey, to be ready for every good work." - Titus 3:1 (CSB).

According to the Scriptures, Satan is the "god of this age" - 2 Corinthians 4:4. The Bible speaks of the world we live in as being evil.

Paul wrote to the Galatians and said, "Grace be to you and peace from God the Father, and from our Lord Jesus Christ, Who gave himself for our sins, that he might deliver us from this present evil world, according to the will of God and our Father." - Galatians 1:3-4 (BRG).

This world and its governments are of Satan's making. He has deceived all nations. - Revelation

12:9. The night before Jesus' crucifixion, He prayed for His followers and said to His Father, "They are not of this world." - John 17:16.

Most governments of this world are in opposition to God in that they are under Satan's sway. Nothing can reform Satan. So, Jesus has to replace him. The same goes for human governments. Jesus is going to replace Satan and the human government!

Christians must say that we must obey God rather than men - Acts 5:29.

Politics are at the center of the story of Jesus. His historical life ended with a political execution. Rome used crucifixion for those who systematically rejected imperial authority.

In essence, Scripture says that you are called to pray for, honor, and submit to governing authorities in a way that allows you to influence others for Christ. The government of Paul and Peter's day persecuted minorities so heavily.

The worst of the persecution was of Christians. It isn't an easy road to follow Jesus in our current times.

Long ago and far away, Jesus predicted that we would be living in a situation where Satan would be looking for ways to entice us.

In the New Testament, Jesus identifies himself with the hungry, the poor, the sick, and the prisoners. - Matthew 25:31-46. Christians are to have this kind of social conscience.

The Bible is a potential weapon of mass destruction. Misusing the Bible in contemporary politics is undeniably destructive to Christianity. History tells us that all empires fell because of that.

Moreover, in the Bible, there runs an anti-imperialist strand, pushing against the hubris and conceit of pharaoh, Babylon, Herod, and Rome.

All their conceit finally failed them. And the systems of power failed because no authority could stand against God.

Christianity is a private matter and not a political one. If we take the lordship of Christ seriously, then we should apply that lordship to our participation in politics. The government shouldn't be confused with the authority behind all authorities.

No political ideology can solve people's problems. The issues that affect the lives of people all over the world are spiritual and require spiritual solutions.

A Christian should be an ambassador of Christ and His coming government - Ephesians 2:1-2 Corinthians 5:20.

Ambassadors of governments must not involve themselves in the politics of other nations.

Christians should do the same as long as the local laws do not conflict with the laws of God - Acts 5:29.

If people are going to follow Jesus' example, they will not get involved in the politics of this world. The politics of Jesus transcend any human political party.

Jesus had good reason to remain apart from politics. The message He preached was about government, but a government He would bring to the earth, not one that would come about through human effort. His message was about the government of God that will rule the world and that will bring about world peace!

So also the heart of his message was political. It was about the coming of "the kingdom of God." These are the first words of Jesus in Mark, the earliest Gospel, an advanced summary of what the Gospel and the story of Jesus are about - Mark 1:14-15.

Of course, Jesus' message was also religious. He was passionate about God and what God was like. That passion led him, in his teaching and actions, to proclaim the kingdom of God.

The kingdom of God is for the earth. The Lord's Prayer speaks of God's kingdom coming on the earth, even as it already exists in heaven. It is about the transformation of this world. What would life be like on earth if God were ruler and the lords of the domination systems were not?

If Jesus had wanted to avoid the political meaning of kingdom language, He could have spoken of the "family" of God, or the "community" of God, or the "people" of God like the many political parties that exist in every country today. But he didn't. He spoke of the kingdom of God.

It would be a world of economic justice in which everybody had the material basics of existence. And it would be a world of peace and non-violence. Together, economic justice and peace are God's passion for a transformed world.

Jesus' passion for the kingdom of God created conflict with the authorities. His public activity began after the arrest of his mentor, John the Baptizer, by the Rome-appointed ruler of Galilee - Mark 1:14.

Conflict dominates His story throughout the Gospels and climaxes in the last week of His life with His challenge to the authorities in Jerusalem and His crucifixion.

His passion for the kingdom of God led to His arrest, suffering, and death. This is the political meaning of Good Friday. Easter also has a political meaning. It meant that God said yes to Jesus' passion for a transformed world and no to the powers of domination that killed him.

Of course, Good Friday and Easter have more than a political meaning, but not less. It may come as a surprise to many, but Jesus Christ did not involve Himself with the politics of His day. Even though He had a strong government interest, He chose not to become involved in any of the political factions of the day, either in the Jewish government or in its overseer, the government of Rome.

Whatever our situation may be, we Christians are not to get involved in the politics of this world. Our mission is to proclaim Christ's message to all nations. The good news is that the Kingdom of God is coming!

# CHAPTER 13

## PRECONCEIVED IDEAS

God wants people to shed their preconceived ideas and follow His commands.

Only the people who Satan is controlling would say in their hearts, 'There is no God.' They might never seek Him because they are corrupt, and their actions are evil; not one of them does good! - Psalm 14:1.

Many of my non-Christian and agnostic friends would ask me why I believe Jesus is the Savior of the world even when scientists and doctors don't do so.

In their case, Satan has blinded their minds to keep them away from seeing the light of the gospel of the glory of Christ that is the image of God - 2 Corinthians 4:4.

However, if they search for the scriptures, they will find Jesus in them.

To search for the scriptures, they must admit that they have preconceived ideas. These ideas hinder them from following Jesus. They keep them away from setting their minds on the things of God. If they want to follow Jesus, then they must shed their preconceived ideas. Their minds must be receptive to the word of God and not deceptive. With skepticism, they cannot learn the Bible truths.

"Then Jesus said unto His disciples, If any man will come after Me, let him deny himself and take up his cross and follow Me." - Matthew 16:24 (KJ21).

So, check out your preconceived ideas to see if they are hindering you from following Jesus. You may have some preconceived notions about the word of God. You need to be more aware of that.

Even the people that lived in the days of Jesus didn't understand the scriptures. There may be some things that you are missing. So, you must beware of your preconceived ideas.

Peter convicted Jews, saying that their preconceived ideas kept them from knowing that Jesus was Christ - Acts 3:17-18.

Listen to what Jesus tells you about Himself. The Pharisees did listen to Him. Yet, they were so rigid in their preconceived ideas that they rejected Him.

If you hold a misconception, you'll never know that your ideas and beliefs are incorrect. For example, if you accepted the ideas beforehand that the religion of your family and society is true, you might never change it. Nevertheless, you are wrong in worshiping a creature of God rather than the Creator Himself - Romans 1:25.

To address your misconception, you must have contact with God. He can help you out in any situation, even though preconceived ideas are hard to change.

You shouldn't be self-confident with your first impressions of anyone. Once you have branded someone with your preconceived ideas, they will always seem like that whenever you see them.

# CHAPTER 14

If you are claiming to walk as Christ walked, you mustn't do what unbelievers do. If you are claiming to be followers of Christ, you must have His Spirit; if you have the Holy Spirit, you must bear the fruit of Him - Galatians 5:22-23.

Many Christians today don't have the fruit of the Holy Spirit. It shows that the Spirit of God is absent in their hearts and minds. If so, how can they get His purposes accomplished? By no means.

We love Him because He first loved us. If you say, 'You love God, and yet hate your fellow Christian, you are a liar. If you don't love your fellow Christian whom you have seen, how can you love God whom you have not seen?' - 1 John 4:19-20.

If you say you are Christian, you must follow the example of Christ - 1 John 2:6.

When I was growing up, I used to believe that all Christians are loving. They focus on the unpleasant things that happen every day. But ever since I heard and saw many Christians killing each other, not to speak of hating each other, I don't believe so anymore.

One reason why there's a lot of denominations in Christendom is that the leaders struggle for control. We all know the story of God throwing Lucifer out of heaven. Isaiah 14:12-14; Revelation 12:7-9.

Dear friends, don't believe everyone who claims to have the Spirit of God. Test them all to find out if they do come from God. Many false prophets have already gone out into the world - 1 John 4:1 (CEV).

Even Satan tries to look like an angel of light - 2 Corinthians 11:14.

But whatever the case may be, only the people who do God's WILL will go to heaven - Matthew 7:15-23; Revelation 22:14-15.

# CHAPTER 15

## SATAN

"Satan sowed tares and evil doctrine - Matthew 13:25,30; Luke 22:31."

I want to stress that most of the 8 billion people on the planet are Satan's human agents. Even the people who you are with are his minions as long as they are non-Christians, atheists, and Christians without the love of Christ. Of course, only the people that have Jesus' love are safe and secure, no matter whether they are Christians or not. So, we'd better be very careful who to be with every day.

Today, most Christians, non-Christians, and agnostics continually live under Satan's power. He is a lion that is constantly seeking to devour faithful Christians. Satan is a person. He is involved in our lives. He is involved in the church. He is involved in politics. He is endeavoring to destroy your testimony, to sidetrack you, to derail you from serving Christ in any capacity that is in any way effective. But the Spirit of God is endeavoring to enable you to live for Christ.

Satan is a reality. He has over six thousand years of experience. Anybody who plays into his hands is playing into a situation where he will do nothing but kill and steal and destroy careless people. He tried to destroy even Christ. Immediately after Christ's baptism, the Spirit of God led Him into the wilderness to confront Satan. Satan tried to derail Him. Satan figured that He wanted the kingdoms of the world. He said to Jesus, 'If You just bow down to me, I'll give them to You. You won't die.' He tried to distract Christ at the very beginning.

He is hostile to God. On one occasion, he even spoke through Peter's mouth. He is a malignant reality. He is always hostile to God and His people. He is always promoting filth and vice and sin. He has no mask. He is a living, active, violent, anti-

God personal being. And he's running this world, in case you didn't know it. He is the prince of this world, the god of this world, and the ruler of this present world. The whole world lies in his hands, like a sleeping baby. And just as God is for you, Satan is against you. That's his job.

The Bible tells us that he is a person, a spirit like God. He is not a human being. He is not self-existent. He was a created being. Ever since his first rebellion against God, he has been in a constant rebellion against his Creator.

Dear friend, if you don't know Jesus Christ as the Savior of the world, I say this with a breaking heart: Satan has bound you. He has blinded your mind to the things of God. And I'm praying that God will open your eyes to see the reality of Jesus Christ today and that you'll know that He died for you.

You may think, 'How can I let Him open my eyes to see Jesus?' Perhaps you can invite Jesus Christ into your life. You can do it right here right now. All you have to do is just say, 'Lord Jesus, come into my heart. Forgive my sin, and take over control of my life.' Why don't you pray right now in your heart?

Dear friend, if Jesus Christ isn't really in your life, and if you don't know that He's your personal Savior, just say, 'Lord Jesus, come into my heart.

Forgive my sin, and take over my life.' He'll do it. He always does so because that's His promise. Invite Him right now and be a part of His glorious Kingdom.

# CHAPTER 16

## NEPOTISM

Nepotism is one of the things that I hate the most. I didn't do anything that goes with it in my life and never will because it causes trouble. I have always heard and also seen many partial people showing nepotism to their family members, relatives, and friends, and that many others lost their careers, jobs, even their lives due to that factor. Almost everybody knows that nepotism is a form of favoritism that people give only to their family members, relatives, and friends in various activities.

The earthly governments don't always do the right things unless they have the Holy Spirit, like defending the citizens from harm and putting an end to insecurity in towns, cities, villages, and any other parts of the world so that everyone can attain greatness. Nepotism causes misgovernance in terms of security, economy, and distribution of goods and services.

Nepotism results in crimes. Such acts of nepotism and favoritism are the prelude to genocide and ethnic cleansing. Crimes are actionable under international human rights and humanitarian law. But in today's money-controlling and running world, hardly any leader can take action against a criminal!

The truth about our earthly government is that there are only two parties now existing: the good and the evil, the oppressed and the oppressor, the suffering people and the benefiting government officers and their families. However, we should never allow Satan's lies to mislead us.

If you ever accuse someone of nepotism, it means that you don't support nepotism. There are laws against nepotism. But even when it is legal, it carries the stain of unearned privilege and corruption. That's why nepotism is a dangerous thing.

You could argue that nepotism is the basis of human civilization. Most of us humans, tend to grant favors to our family members and not to people who aren't related to us. This habit turns out to have deep roots in our human nature. It's worth taking a closer look at nepotism's biological origins, cultural history, and the measurable effect it has on us.

When we hear the word nepotism, distressing images of the unqualified and undeserving come to our minds. It's a natural segue into a discussion about how it is not what you know but who you know.

But the fact is, nepotism stands as a common practice that occurs in companies, movie industries, athletics, debates, exams, authorities, employment opportunities, associations, non-profit organizations, civil society organizations, security forces, and small businesses. And despite its negative impacts, it sometimes helps make a more sustainable business model.

For many reasons, hiring a family member or a relative makes sense because you are probably more familiar with a family members' strengths, weaknesses, and potential than you are with other candidates. They offer swift trust so that you can rely on them when it comes to sensitive information and confidential aspects of your business. They likely share the same values and mission as you, with a vested interest in seeing you and your business succeed.

But nepotism can lead you into dangerous territory, thus sending a ripple effect of resentment and frustration throughout a joint effort. Before you hire a family member, you must understand that people tend to believe that favoritism occurs if you hire a relative, regardless of their stance on nepotism.

Even when a relative may be uniquely qualified for the job, coworkers often think that it was their familial ties, not their resume or college degrees, that got them the position.

Nepotism is particularly problematic if it comes to higher positions for others because there's no way that they can achieve.

But whatever it may be, God doesn't allow nepotism.

We can see it in these scriptures, such as 1 Samuel 3:10-14; Numbers 3:1-51; James 2:9; Leviticus 19:36; Luke 6:27; Romans 2:1; Ephesians 6:9; Acts 10:34; Deuteronomy 10:17.

# CHAPTER 17

## SELFISHNESS

"The love of God is not found in selfishness - John 3:17; Romans 15: 1-3."

Dear friend, the Holy Spirit dictated that I write a few points on selfishness as well. Many people today are selfish and greedy. So, if you are curious about the things that the Holy Spirit wanted me to write, please read on until you're through.

Jesus never did anything for Himself, only for others, while on earth. Neither did His disciples except for Judas Iscariot. Selfishness is the act of seeking one's advantage, pleasure, or well-being without regard for others.

There are several examples of selfish people in the Bible from which we all can learn valuable lessons. One of the Biblical aspects of selfishness is Cain killing his brother Abel selfishly.

Selfishness makes it easier for us to fall into traps like an addiction.

Our selfishness can show that we hurt others as we ruthlessly strive to satisfy our own needs. The selfish attitude of David caused him to seek fulfillment of his pleasures with no regard to the cost of getting them.

We humans tend to withdraw our love and affection from someone when they behave selfishly. Selfish actions hurt us. So, we get protective and defensive. But God's love is unconditional, and even our disobedience cannot separate us from His love. For instance, He showed Jonah love even when Jonah's behavior was defiant.

Most people today are selfishly pursuing pleasure with no regard for either consequences or the impact of their actions upon others. However, God expects us to show concern for each other.

Evil and social chaos are rapidly intensifying across the globe due to selfishness. The Bible says that evildoers and impostors will go from bad to worse. Many signs or events that Jesus said would take place before His return are taking place.

Many security armed forces tend to kill civilians and non-civilians in cold blood, in fake encounters, without ever showing any respect to Human Rights. They also violate females and murder them, and provide false evidence. They do all these sinful things to get gallantry awards, promotions, personal fame, money, etc.

Even some male friends violate and strangle their female friends and leave them behind as if they had committed suicide. And some friends murder their friends because they don't want successful friends to be the best in everything and because they are so jealous of their friends' possessions, such as good looks, abilities, qualities, and accomplishments. And they fabricate evidence to make it seem like they have committed suicide.

Nowadays, people are afraid to speak the truth for fear of losing their career, job, life, and therefore remain quiet when people commit crimes against others or even against their extended family members. People kill anyone else who speaks the truth. It just goes on to show that this world is about to end. And the days of Satan's rebellion are just about over, and he knows it.

That's why he is constantly using many people to kill people and is trying to get as many people as possible to do anything that is against God's WILL.

Dear friend, if you want to be in the mighty hands of Christ at all times until He comes, make it your goal to be faithful to Him no matter what happens around you.

# CHAPTER 18

## SUICIDE

Suicide is something that almost happened to me years ago. The Holy Spirit moved me to share it with you, friend.

I tried to hang myself on a Gulmohar tree that grows in front of my parents' house when I was 12 years old because I had nothing to survive for. Two of my older sisters saw me tying the rope to a branch of the tree to hang myself. They pleaded with me not to ever do that if I loved them.

I didn't want to break their hearts, so I decided not to commit suicide.

I lived among people, but I felt as if I lived amid wild animals because I didn't see Jesus in any of them and still haven't seen Him in many of them. Life seemed to be meaningless. Little did I know how much Jesus loves me and cares about me. Ever since the still small voice told me that, I have considered my poor self very much more valuable than the things of this world.

I have a unique way of thinking: as long as I have Christ, I have hope and life. Without Him, there is no meaning in my life. I never did anything sinful and hurtful after I found the truth in Him and never deliberately will. I know enough to say that Satan can easily deceive those who don't worship Jesus into committing suicide even when they may not seem to lack anything in physical life.

That may be one reason I am not up to everybody's expectations. I know that many great people in the world have family and friends' support. That's one reason they come across as being extraordinary and successful in physical life.

My family members, relatives, neighbors, and friends always tell me that I have wasted most of my time and energy living for Christ. They say so because they don't see what He has in store for me in heaven above. They often even tell me that Jesus will never drop anything good for me down from the sky.

They say so because they have no idea what He promised to do for His people.

On my part, I only ever try to make them understand the Bible truths by sharing the word and love of Christ with them every time the opportunity presents itself.

# CHAPTER 19

## SCAM

"There is no salvation in scamming people. Proverbs 10:2-3."

My local friends who know English would describe me as a walking-talking English dictionary. But I wasn't quite familiar with the word 'scam' until recently because I took it for granted.

My family and I live among the most non-Christians and the least encouraging Christians in a far-flung part of India. I like to make friends with faithful and helpful Christians from all over the world to support me physically and spiritually.

So, I would send friend requests to international Pastors, Christian leaders, and Christian individuals.

Almost everyone would ask me in their replies if I was looking to scam them rather than accept my request.

Unfortunately, I would have bad times with their unChristian words and even their blocking me.

Then, I would share my situation with some new people, and they would tell me that many strangers had scammed them and therefore they weren't interested in connecting with strangers anymore.

However, thank God, I could secure the confidence and friendship of some of them.

That's how the word scam became a part of my mastered English vocabulary.

To meet good brothers and sisters in Christ, I would say this prayer when getting online:

'Thank You so much, Lord, for this opportunity to get online and benefit from it. Lord, please introduce me to good people who I can befriend and with whom to share the love of Your Son Jesus. And thank You again, Lord, for answering my prayer. In Jesus' mighty name, I pray, Amen!'

Anyway, I am so thankful to God for positive-thinkers and negative-thinkers! Those who blocked me and those who accepted my requests are real blessings to me because I got to learn new lessons from both.

# CHAPTER 20

## PEACE AND SECURITY

"Jesus is the source of peace - John 14:27; Philippians 4:7."

I wanted to tell you, friend, just a little of what I have always felt about these two things in my heart.

Peace and security are among the things that the word of God encourages me to share with my family and everyone else I meet every day. We humans love these things. So, we try to promote them to one another. All religions teach them to their members, but only a few have them.

Many things in life unnecessarily rob us of our sense of peace and security. For example, the coronavirus scares us away. We can't go free anywhere anymore.

Of course, this covid pandemic is a sign of the times of the end. Without Christ, we have no safety in this world.

Every country takes up preventive measures against all kinds of evil. Every leader makes tall talks that they will get rid of these crises. However, they can't do everything.

It is undeniably true that Satan has blinded the people who don't accept Jesus as the Savior of the world, and even many Christians, to God's WILL. I wish that everyone in the world kept saying, 'Cast all your burdens unto Jesus'! Not everyone hears the same statement.

The whole world today says the message, 'Stay home, stay safe during Covid-19 lockdown.' That means that they don't have Jesus! Nevertheless, I am most encouraged that many Christians commit their lives to Him every day.

The Bible tells us that Jesus gives us joy, peace, and security. Not only that, but also He gives us everlasting life.

The whole world should understand that we belong to Him and not to ourselves and therefore we don't need to worry about anything in life because He is the One who offers good care of our lives.

# CHAPTER 21

Dear friends,

I had never imagined in my mind about getting this moment to share my story in writing because we lived a foolish local traditional life. We didn't have any contact with the outside world, nor did we have a phone or anything like that.

Today, I am so grateful to share the love of Jesus with anybody on the planet. The fact is, I am so thankful to God that He has shown me very clearly how much He loves my poor family and lets us join His heavenly family.

My name is Somila. I was born on March 14,1992, as the first daughter and as the eldest child of Ngashanpam Kasar and Khayawon Kasar. I belong to the Tangkhul tribe. We are five siblings. I have two younger brothers and two younger sisters. One

*Somila, my wife.*

brother named Noah is just after me. Then, two sisters in a row (named, Chonchon and Chanchan), and then the youngest brother (named, Vareshang).

Sadly, my parents lost my dear brother Noah this year due to having little money to get him to a doctor or hospital. He struggled with some excruciating pain in his stomach for two weeks. He kept crying due to extreme abdominal pain every day.

He sang praises to God and said prayers during his sickness every day.

A local physician told my parents to take him to the nearest hospital immediately. They didn't have enough money for medications and others. So, they didn't go for any medical treatments.

My husband Canary and I reminded them of God's promises and provisions. So, my father and his friends were traveling toward Imphal after they carried Noah on their backs for ten miles in the mountains one after the other on the night of July 21, 2022.

They reached Imphal at 11:30 PM.

The next day, he passed away at 10: 30 AM. He lived in this world for 25 years. He didn't want to die. So, he prayed three times on his hospital bed before he died.

He made many plans to do great things for God's glory and honor through Shepherd's House Ministry.

Some people are speculating that the doctors might have injected him wrong drugs. He didn't have any chronic health issues. Only recently, he had sudden stomach pain and fever. His dead body turned purple a few minutes after he stopped breathing. But we just believe that God called him to be with Him.

We're so satisfied that he got opportunities to pray three times before he crossed over! Not many people got time to pray before death.

I could say that our life is nothing more than of insects compared to the lives of privileged backgrounds. It can be gone at any time.

I was growing up in the mountains amid wild animals and bugs. That's why I didn't get to see the advanced life of man for so long. That's why I didn't get formal education for so long. That's why I didn't even dream about the mechanical things of mind-blowing science and technology that most humans are using today.

Here in the hills and mountains, people eat, live, and die almost like wild animals. Nobody can live a meaningful life because it is too far to live. I come from such a beastly, meaningless environment.

However, I do believe that God brought me into this world for a purpose. My father's eldest brother and his family moved to a municipal town where there are schools.

In the year 2003, they came to get my formal education there despite their hand-to-mouth life. My parents, relatives, and all other members of my extended family live in difficult circumstances.

By God's grace, I did reasonably well in school even though I started my schooling too late. That too, in a cheap school of which teaching method wasn't up to scratch.

An ethnic conflict occurred between two tribes while I was in Grade 10. So, my uncle got me back to my parents.

At that time, my mother was bedridden with malaria.

There was nobody to cook food for my sick mother and my siblings when my father fished in rivers and hunted animals for a livelihood.

Because of that, I hadn't gone back to my uncle's for my schooling. I was bitterly disappointed with it. I started studying in Grade 5 and on to Grade 10. I went to school only five years in my life.

Finally, I thought to myself,' God sent me to school for only five years just so that I can read and write His word.'

As to my marital status, Leivon Canary Kom and I started a family life as husband and wife on February 15, 2011, as per God's plan. He has endowed us with four precious sons: Matthew, Mark, Baruch, and Samuel.

We didn't want to have that many children. We are so poor, and we cannot afford to get their physical needs. Yet, God has entrusted four children to us for His kingdom, and His word always reminds us that He is our Provider and Savior. - Philippians 4:19; 2 Samuel 22:3.

Humanly speaking, we don't have anything material except for some old clothes and utensils. We live like nomads. We don't have a home to live in, nor do we have a Church to worship God.

However, God never fails to give us our urgent needs: temporary shelter, food, clothing, and medicine. He always provides for our needs in different ways and not our wants.

The bigger picture that He has so far shown us is that He always looks down upon my humble family from His throne of grace He led us to Mom Barbara and Aunt Brenda and their amazing families and friends. We're so blessed to be sharing in their physical and spiritual journey!

We are most faithful that He will give us a home to glorify His name and a Church to worship Him in His perfect timing.

Dear friends, I still have so much more to tell you about my life and family, but anyway, I am looking forward to doing more another time.

Now, as I wrap up my story, I'd like to ask you all to keep my husband, sons, and extended families in your prayers.

Thanks so much for the time, and God bless you abundantly!

# CHAPTER 22

My name is Leivon Alen Kom. I belong to North-East India. I was born in a nonChristian family on March 1, 1950, as the second son of late Mr. Leivon Ringlersong Kom and late Mrs. Leivon Bomkhupning Kom, the residents of Tuiringphaisan village, Churachandpur District, Manipur, India.

I didn't study systematically well because my poor parents couldn't afford to send me to a school for the one-year session. I went to school at irreg-

*Leivon Alen Kom, my father.*

ular intervals of time. By God's grace, I somehow managed to study until I graduated.

My Kom tribal culture, poor circumstances, and animism blinded us from the civilization of the other human beings. Almost nobody ever tried to live a better life. Everybody stepped into the shoes of their ancestors. Even today, most people still practice everything that their forefathers did.

I remember when the locals used to say that Christianity was an English religion because it was introduced here by the English people for the first time in history. And most of them still say so. I was one of those vicious people.

At age fifteen, I began using intoxicants, such as alcohol, betelnuts, tobacco products, and cigarettes through peer pressure.

In 1952, my parents accepted Jesus as the Savior of the world and got the baptism under the care of an American Baptist Mission. But I didn't follow the religion that they followed. They were stalwart Christians. They would pray for me all the time.

I married Sumtinnei Kom on July 5, 1969. My wife took the Christian faith through my parents. My parents-in-law and I were still in the dark about the Bible truths. My in-laws didn't encourage Christianity. So, on March 7, 1972, we moved to Mahou Tera village. I still live here today. I have seven children (four sons and three daughters).

On the night of January 30, 2004, I had an unprecedented dream. It was of the second coming of Jesus Christ. Heaven's door opened on the western side. Jesus and His angels came down with trumpet sounds and glory. Many people were welcoming them with thanksgiving and hymns. Many others were asking for the forgiveness of their sins. Just then, I repented for fear of hellfire.

But I was too late to find favor in Christ, though. Out of so much fear, I woke up from my sleep. It was all a dream! That very night, I quit all of my bad habits.

According to God's plan, my wife crossed over this world on December 8, 2015. That was the most shocking and tearful moment of my life when nobody and nothing could comfort me except for God's word. With her untimely passing away, a huge hole is in my heart and always will be. However, the Bible fills this vacuum.

I fervently believe that my ability to overcome evil was the answer to my son Canary who consistently prayed for me. Ever since the beginning of my new life, I have been asking God to enable me to do something for His kingdom.

Suddenly, on April 9, 2021, a package of Bibles arrived at my home for my son Canary. I saw it as a miracle because then I had been praying for a Bible. An American lady named Barbara Hemphill Taylor sent it. She has sent 89 Bibles so far. More boxes of Bibles are on the way. I have greater joy planting the seeds of truth into the minds of my close friends, thus distributing the Bibles.

Today, I do God's ministry like Paul walking from village to village for miles and miles. I will be doing it as long as I live.

# CHAPTER 23

My beloved Christian family members scattered all over the world,

Greetings to you all so far away from Northeast India!

Today, I am so abundantly blessed to share some bits of my life stories with the outside world through Leivon Canary Kom, my granddaughter

*RK Ismael, my wife's grandfather.*

Somila's husband! I have so many stories combined with sadness and happiness that other people will find too hard to believe! But I must admit that all those things are the spices of being a true child of God.

My name is RK Ismael. I live in a remote, rural hill village settled in the furthest northeastern part of India. I belong to the Tangkhul tribe. I was born in 1950 as the first son and second child of Mr. Panshu RK and Mrs. Sharphangla RK, Tora village, Ukhrul District.

I feel somewhat dissatisfied with my birth details! My parents didn't keep them in writing for me because they were illiterate. I also didn't try to memorize them.

As I shared my life stories with my granddaughter Somila and her husband Canary, I didn't have enough details of them to mention. I regret not having them all! Even then, I told them all that I had as a way to glorify the name of Jesus.

When I was little, I hoped to be a Pastor. But God has a different plan for me. I am now 71 years old. The fact is, He didn't give me everything that I asked Him.

My parents accepted Christ as the Savior of the world even though they didn't know how to read His word.

There were also no Tangkhul Bibles to read out to them back then. The Holy Spirit worked in them, listened to the ones that brought the gospel to them, and understood God's word. I believe that their minds were receptive enough to listen to His word. They never read a Bible in their lifetime. But they accepted Christ as the Savior of the world that many literate people didn't believe Him.

My parents and some other Christians would worship Jesus in caves to avoid being punished by the devil-worshipping king of the village. All the villagers were under his despotic rule. No one was supposed to be stubborn against his orders. My forefathers were animists.

I didn't take any formal education in my life because my parents were too poor to send me to a school. But later on, by God's grace, I got the literacy from some friends who also picked up the skills from their friends. I believe that the Spirit of God gave me this literacy to glorify His name. I got the baptism in 1963.

In 1971, I married Mingthingla, D/O Mr. Khavangshing Kashung, and Mrs. Thishanla Khashung, Zingshong, Senapati District. We had 7 children.

My wife and first son are gone to be with Jesus. My first son, named Yangmasho died, due to sickness. We hadn't given him enough medical treatment because we were so poor.

My wife's parents were wealthy enough to eat and drink extravagantly in the village. Her father was the king of Zingshong village. So, they made me and my wife live close to them.

Because they lived a life of eat-drink-and-enjoy-before-you-die, they had squandered all their possessions very soon. At last, they became poor and died under so many difficulties. They didn't leave any valuable materials for us.

Even today, I still live alone in a hut in my wife's village after everyone has gone to their different ways. The same prayer that I continue to pray after my wife went to be with Jesus in heaven is, 'Lord, please use the rest of my life in building Your kingdom.'

One thing that I want to mention here is that God showed me a miracle on October 26, 2021, after I prayed for a Tangkhul Bible. I never knew that God would give me the Bible through my granddaughter Somila and her husband Canary, which came from sister Barbara Hemphill Taylor, Raleigh, NC. Hallelujah! God has different ways to provide for His loved ones!

As I conclude my brief testimony, I want to thank Canary, my grandson-in-law, for writing it in English and for telling me that he is going to share it with the whole world to glorify God's name. Well, I am hereby sending lots of love and blessings to you all who have read my testimony in the amazing name of Christ Jesus, Amen!

# CONCLUSION

The continued covid pandemic lockdown made us quite helpless and restless. But finally, God showed Himself to us through a LinkedIn friend on April 24, 2020, at 12:48 AM.

She is none other than Barbara Hemphill Taylor, North Carolina. My wife and I consider her as our spiritual Mom. Our children call her Granny. We are so thankful to God that everything in our physical and spiritual life has changed into meaningful, purposeful, hopeful, and joyful beings ever since we met her! She's the one that gave us hope to live a physical and spiritual life in parallel, leading us from hopeless situations through hopeful situations.

We are beyond blessed and honored to be part of her amazing family and her friend Brenda Quine Heintzelman and other good friends!

Indeed, she is an angel that God sent to us during the Covid-19 lockdown!

The word goes around that 2020 was the worst year in history, but that is not the case because everything happens for a reason.

So, now, in conclusion, I would like to say that we should get closer to God day by day so that His kingdom gets closer to us.

Let's fight together for the truth, my friend.

It is my hope and prayer that we will have the total triumph over Satan and his aides, then sing a song of deliverance, and live together with Christ in the Promised Land forever and ever. Amen!

FOLLOW CANARY ON

# Facebook

# COME BUILD WITH US!

The **Shepherd's House Ministry** is a project in Northeast India **prompted by God** and initiated by **Barbara Hemphill** through **Global Hope India.**

Its purpose is to be a home, entrepreneurial development center, and gathering place for sharing the Gospel of Jesus Christ.

"For every house is built by someone, but the builder of all things is God."
Hebrews 3:4 (ESV)

## WE INVITE YOU TO
# GIVE & CONNECT!

 **www.givesendgo.com/shepherdshouse**

 **Shepherd's House Ministry**

INVITE BARBARA TO SHARE WITH YOUR CHURCH, BUSINESS, OR GROUP ABOUT

# THE SHEPHERD'S HOUSE MINISTRY.

BARBARAHEMPHILL.COM

AS FEATURED IN

USA TODAY

CNN tonight

Guideposts

REALSIMPLE

FAST COMPANY

GOOD MORNING AMERICA

NBC

The New York Times

Made in the USA
Middletown, DE
11 February 2023

24629293R00068